MW01634503

Classic
SPANISH

Classic SPANISH

Authentic regional recipes from all over Spain

FOREWORD BY

SILVANA FRANCO

This edition published in 1998 by Hermes House

Hermes House is an imprint of
Anness Publishing Limited
Hermes House, 88-89 Blackfriars Road, London SE1 8HA

ISBN 1-84038-010-1

Publisher Joanna Lorenz
Senior Cookery Editor Linda Fraser
In-house Editor Anne Hildyard
Designer Nigel Partridge
Illustrations Madeleine David
Photographers Karl Adamson, Steve Baxter, James Duncan, Michelle Garrett and Michael Michaels
Recipes Catherine Atkinson, Jacqueline Clark, Roz Denny, Joanna Farrow, Sarah Gates, Shirley Gill, Sue Maggs, Liz Trigg and Steven Wheeler
Food for photography Jane Hartshorn, Wendy Lee and Jane Stevenson
Jacket photography Amanda Heywood

Printed and bound in Singapore

3 5 7 9 10 8 6 4 2

For all recipes, quantities are given in both metric and imperial measures, and, where appropriate, measures are also given in standard cups and spoons. Follow one set, but not a mixture, because they are not interchangeable.

Pictures on frontispiece, pages 7, 8 and 9: Zefa Picture Library Ltd.

Contents

Foreword

The Spanish take their food seriously: so seriously in fact, that the whole day's business revolves around the day's meals. Starting with a breakfast – which commonly consists of coffee with pastries – through mid-morning snacks to lunch, when shops and work places close until at least 4pm while four-course lunches are followed by afternoon siestas. And at the end of the working day, it's on to the tapas bar for a few glasses of sherry and the odd delicious morsel. Without doubt, a meal is more often than not a social occasion.

The food of Spain is one of the most exciting and varied cuisines of Europe. Its colourful and romantic history has bestowed on Spain an eclectic blend of styles encompassing many flavoursome regional ingredients, such as the delicious ewe's milk cheese *Manchego* and salt-cured ham *jamón serrano*. The regions each have their own very characteristic cuisines stretching from the Basque region in the northernmost corner, which is considered to be the home of Spain's most sophisticated cookery and finest chefs, down to Andalusia – the land of the olive and the grape.

And now, Spanish food, having found its feet in restaurants and tapas bars across the globe, is fast becoming familiar in everyday British kitchens, alongside the readily accepted cuisines of Italy and France.

This wonderful book captures the spirit of Spain with a wide selection of classics such as Gazpacho, *Zarzuela* and Crema Catalana. It makes great use of traditional ingredients such as the fabulously spicy sausage, chorizo, and offers authentic dishes which are ideal for any occasion.

Classic Spanish is packed with helpful tips, the recipes are all easy to master, and they give fantastic results, so don't be afraid to take the bull by the horns!

Silvana Franco

Introduction

There are few countries where food is enjoyed with greater relish than Spain. In Madrid, the gastronomic hub of the country, you can sample cooking from every corner of this fascinating land, beginning at breakfast with *Churros* – spirals of delectable deep-fried batter introduced by Arab invaders – and often ending only at midnight, with a creamy caramel dessert after a satisfying dinner. In between, the *Madrileño*, who rises early, will eat a light lunch (*almuerzo*) at around 11am, then return to work to build up his appetite for the *comida* – a main meal served at around 2.30pm. This will probably consist of at least three courses: perhaps a colourful Roasted Pepper Soup, then a robust fish, meat or game dish and finally a bowl of sweet strawberries from Catalonia, sprinkled with orange juice from the same region.

Not surprisingly, a siesta is essential after such a superb meal, but it will soon be time for coffee and pastries before the evening work begins. After that, a few tapas dishes in a friendly bar will set the scene for the final meal of the day, at around 10pm.

Elsewhere in the country, the pattern is similar, although the meals are generally lighter in the south, especially in the hot months, when fish in a crisp light batter is likely to be on the menu, along with that freshest of all summer soups – Gazpacho. Sometimes referred to as liquid salad, this is a rich red tomato soup, served lightly chilled, with a selection of garnishes such as chopped cucumber and green pepper.

The east coast is famous for its fish and shellfish, including squid, clams, lobsters, mussels, anchovies and sardines. Here, too, you will encounter rice paddies and fields of crocuses, the stamens of which yield saffron. Small wonder that Valencia is the home of Seafood Paella, the wonderful mixture of saffron-flavoured rice, monkfish, mullet, prawns, mussels, peas and the bright sweet red peppers that also grow in this region.

Another unmissable seafood dish is *Zarzuela*, a vibrant combination of the best of that morning's catch, served in a richly flavoured sauce spiked with brandy.

Men do much of the cooking in Spain, particularly in the Basque region, where groups of gourmets will often gather to share their favourite dishes. These mellow gatherings, not often open to outsiders, are where some of the finest food in all Spain is consumed.

Nearby Aragon is known for its sauces, especially the famous *chilindron*, made from roasted peppers, tomatoes, onion, garlic and ham and served with chicken, veal and rabbit.

Game is popular throughout Spain, with the wild boar a particular favourite. Pork is widely eaten, often as sucking pig, or as the principal ingredient in chorizo, a smoked sausage flavoured with paprika and garlic. Chorizo appears in many of the recipes in this collection, as a stuffing for dates, in a salad with broad beans and mushrooms and as a flavouring in a hearty Black Bean Stew. Desserts range from the rich sweetmeats of the south, a legacy of the Moorish invasion, to fresh fruits, especially melons, peaches, apricots and oranges.

To sample the best that Spain has to offer, simply turn the page and take a cook's tour in the comfort of your own home!

A spectacular mountain range in Catalonia (left) and a colourful market in Barcelona, displaying a tempting array of fruit and vegetables (right).

ROASTED PEPPER SOUP

Grilling intensifies the flavour of sweet red and yellow peppers and gives this delicious soup its stunning, vibrant colour.

INGREDIENTS

3 red peppers
1 yellow pepper
1 onion, chopped
1 garlic clove, crushed
750ml/1¼ pints/3 cups vegetable stock
15ml/1 tbsp plain flour
salt and ground black pepper
60ml/4 tbsp red and yellow peppers, diced, to garnish

SERVES 4

1 Preheat the grill. Halve the peppers and remove the stalks and white pith. Scrape out the seeds.

2 Line a grill pan with foil and arrange the halved peppers, skin-side up, in a single layer. Grill until the skins have blackened and blistered.

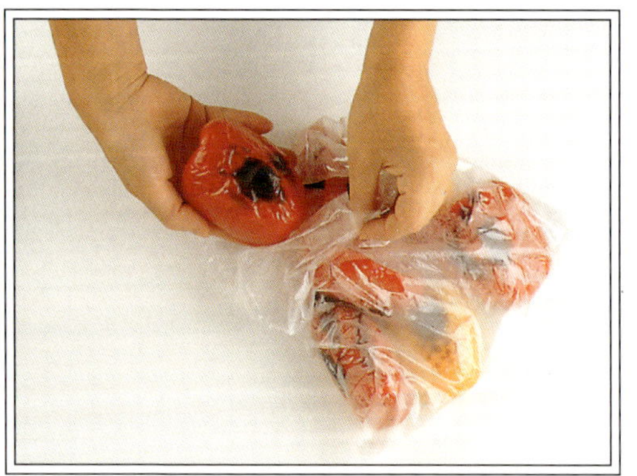

3 Transfer the grilled peppers to a plastic bag and leave until cool. Then peel away the skins, under cold running water, and throw away. Roughly chop the flesh.

4 Put the onion, garlic and 150ml/¼ pint/⅔ cup stock into a large saucepan. Bring to the boil and boil for 5 minutes until most of the stock has reduced. Lower the heat and stir until the onion is softened and just beginning to colour.

5 Sprinkle the flour over the onions, then gradually stir in the remaining stock. Add the chopped, roasted peppers and bring to the boil. Cover and simmer for a further 5 minutes.

6 Remove from the heat and leave to cool slightly, then purée in a blender or food processor until smooth. Season to taste with salt and ground black pepper. Return to the saucepan and reheat the soup until piping hot. Ladle into four soup plates and garnish each with a sprinkling of diced peppers.

GAZPACHO

This classic no-cook soup is ideal for taking on picnics as it can be packed straight from the fridge. Keep the chopped vegetables in separate bowls and hand them round for people to help themselves.

INGREDIENTS

1 slice white bread, crusts removed
1 garlic clove
30ml/2 tbsp extra virgin olive oil
30ml/2 tbsp white wine vinegar
6 large ripe tomatoes, skinned and finely chopped
1 small onion, finely chopped
2.5ml/½ tsp paprika
pinch of ground cumin
150ml/¼ pint/⅔ cup tomato juice
salt and ground black pepper

TO GARNISH

1 green pepper, seeded and chopped
½ cucumber, peeled, seeded and chopped

FOR THE CROUTONS

2 slices bread, cubed and deep fried

SERVES 6

1 Soak the slice of bread in enough cold water just to cover and leave for about 5 minutes, then mash with a fork.

2 Pound the garlic, oil and vinegar using a pestle and mortar, or purée in a blender or food processor. Then stir this mixture into the bread.

3 Spoon the mixture into a large bowl and stir in the tomatoes, onion, spices and tomato juice. Season, then chill. Make the garnishes and croûtons.

4 To serve, ladle the soup into six chilled soup plates and then hand round the garnishes and croûtons separately.

ALMOND SOUP

Unless you want to spend time pounding the ingredients for this dish by hand, a blender or food processor is essential. It's very simple and wonderfully refreshing to eat on a hot day.

INGREDIENTS

115g/4oz fresh white bread
115g/4oz/1 cup blanched almonds
2 garlic cloves, sliced
75ml/5 tbsp olive oil
25ml/1½ tbsp sherry vinegar
salt and ground black pepper
toasted flaked almonds and a few seedless green and black grapes, skinned and halved, to garnish

SERVES 6

1 Break the bread into a bowl and pour over 150ml/¼ pint/⅔ cup cold water. Leave for 5 minutes.

2 Process the almonds and garlic in a blender or food processor until very finely ground. Then blend in the bread.

3 Gradually add the olive oil until the mixture forms a smooth paste. Add the sherry vinegar, then 600ml/1 pint/2½ cups cold water, and process the mixture until absolutely smooth.

4 Turn into a bowl and season with salt and ground black pepper, adding a little more water if the soup is very thick. Chill for at least 2–3 hours.

5 Ladle into soup plates and scatter with toasted flaked almonds and the green and black grapes.

COOK'S TIP

This soup must be served very cold. If liked, add one or two ice cubes to each soup plate to serve.

GALICIAN BROTH

This delicious main course soup is a very warming, chunky meat and vegetable broth. For extra colour, a few onion skins can be added when cooking the gammon, but remember to remove them before serving.

INGREDIENTS

450g/1lb piece gammon
2 bay leaves
2 onions, sliced
10ml/2 tsp paprika
675g/1½lb potatoes, cut into large chunks
225g/8oz spring greens
425g/15oz can haricot or cannellini beans, drained
salt and ground black pepper

SERVES 4

1 Soak the piece of gammon overnight in cold water. Drain and put in a large saucepan with the bay leaves, onions and 1.5 litres/2½ pints/6¼ cups cold water.

2 Bring to the boil then reduce the heat and simmer very gently for about 1½ hours until the meat is tender.

3 Drain the meat, reserving the cooking liquid, and leave to cool slightly. Discard the skin and any excess fat from the meat and cut into small chunks. Return to the pan with the paprika and potatoes. Cover and simmer gently for 20 minutes.

4 Cut away the tough central cores from the spring greens. Roll up the leaves and cut into thin shreds with a very sharp knife. Add to the pan with the beans and simmer for 10 minutes. Season to taste and serve the broth hot.

MUSSEL BISQUE

Served hot, this mussel bisque is a delicious and very filling soup, perfect for lunch. It is equally enjoyable served cold.

INGREDIENTS

675g/1½lb live mussels
75ml/5 tbsp white wine or cider
25g/1oz/2 tbsp butter
1 small red onion, chopped
1 small leek, thinly sliced
1 carrot, finely diced
2 tomatoes, skinned, seeded and chopped
2 garlic cloves, crushed
15ml/1 tbsp chopped fresh parsley
15ml/1 tbsp chopped fresh basil
1 celery stick, finely sliced
½ red pepper, seeded and chopped
250ml/8fl oz/1 cup whipping cream
salt and ground black pepper

SERVES 6

1 Scrub the mussels and pull off the beards. Discard any broken ones, or any that don't close when tapped. Place them in a large pan with the white wine or cider and 150ml/¼ pint/⅔ cup water.

2 Cover the saucepan and cook the mussels over a high heat until all of them are open. (Discard any mussels that don't open.) Using a slotted spoon, transfer the mussels to a dish and leave until cold enough to handle. When the mussels are cooled, cover, and set aside in a cool place until needed.

3 Strain the stock through a piece of muslin or a fine cloth to get rid of any grit. Heat the butter in the same large pan and cook the onion, leek, carrot, tomatoes and garlic over a high heat for 2–3 minutes.

4 Reduce the heat and cook for 3 minutes. Add the stock, 300ml/½ pint/1¼ cups water and the herbs and simmer for 10 minutes. Shell the mussels, and add with the celery, pepper, and cream. Season and serve.

SALT COD BITES WITH GARLIC MAYONNAISE

This is a popular Spanish dish and the salty bites go very well with a strong garlicky mayonnaise. Soak the salt cod thoroughly and do not add any extra salt while preparing the dish.

INGREDIENTS

225g/8oz dried salt cod
675g/1½lb floury potatoes
1 garlic clove, crushed
45ml/3 tbsp chopped fresh parsley
1 egg yolk, beaten
15ml/1 tbsp plain flour
vegetable oil, for deep frying
ground black pepper

FOR THE GARLIC MAYONNAISE

3 garlic cloves, crushed
juice of ½ lemon
300ml/½ pint/1¼ cups mayonnaise

SERVES 4

1 Soak the cod for at least 24 hours, changing the water regularly, to soften the cod and reduce the salt content.

2 Drain well, then break the cod into small pieces, carefully removing any skin or bones from the fish.

3 Cook the potatoes until tender, then drain. Mash with the garlic, parsley and egg yolk.

4 Fold in the cod and season well with pepper. Using floured hands, shape the mixture into 20 walnut-size balls.

5 Heat the oil in a large, heavy-based saucepan until a cube of stale bread sizzles immediately when dropped in. Deep fry the balls in batches for 2 minutes. Drain on kitchen paper and keep warm.

6 For the garlic mayonnaise, whisk together the garlic, lemon juice and mayonnaise. Serve with the hot fish balls.

GARLIC PRAWNS

In Spain, *Gambas al Ajillo* are traditionally cooked in small earthenware dishes, but a frying pan serves just as well.

INGREDIENTS

60ml/4 tbsp olive oil
2–3 garlic cloves, finely chopped
16 cooked whole Mediterranean prawns
15ml/1 tbsp chopped fresh parsley
lemon wedges and French bread, to serve

SERVES 4

1 Heat the oil in a large frying pan and add the garlic. Stir-fry for 1 minute, until the garlic begins to turn brown.

2 Add the Mediterranean prawns and stir-fry for 3–4 minutes, coating them well with the flavoured oil.

3 Add the parsley, remove from the heat and serve four prawns per person in heated bowls, with the flavoured oil spooned over them. Serve with lemon wedges for squeezing and French bread to mop up the delicious juices.

TAPAS OF ALMONDS, OLIVES AND CHEESE

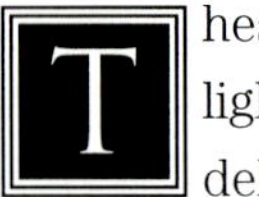

These three simple ingredients are lightly flavoured to create a delicious tapas medley.

INGREDIENTS

FOR THE MARINATED OLIVES

2.5ml/½ tsp coriander seeds
2.5ml/½ tsp fennel seeds
5ml/1 tsp chopped fresh rosemary
10ml/2 tsp chopped fresh parsley
2 garlic cloves, crushed
15ml/1 tbsp sherry vinegar
30ml/2 tbsp olive oil
115g/4oz/⅔ cup each black and green olives

FOR THE MARINATED CHEESE

150g/5oz goat's cheese
90ml/6 tbsp olive oil
15ml/1 tbsp white wine vinegar
5ml/1 tsp black peppercorns
1 garlic clove, sliced
3 sprigs fresh tarragon or thyme

FOR THE SALTED ALMONDS

1.5ml/¼ tsp cayenne pepper
30ml/2 tbsp sea salt
25g/1oz butter
60ml/4 tbsp olive oil
200g/7oz/1¼ cups blanched almonds

SERVES 6–8

1 For the marinated olives, crush the coriander and fennel seeds using a pestle and mortar. Mix together with the herbs, garlic, vinegar and oil and pour over the olives in a small bowl. Cover and chill in the fridge for up to 1 week.

2 For the marinated cheese, cut the cheese into bite-size pieces, leaving the rind on. Place in a small bowl. Mix together the oil, wine vinegar, peppercorns, garlic and sprigs of tarragon or thyme. Pour over the cheese Cover the bowl and chill in the fridge for up to 3 days.

3 For the salted almonds, mix together the cayenne pepper and sea salt in a bowl. Melt the butter with the olive oil in a frying pan. Add the almonds and fry quite gently, stirring, for about 5 minutes, or until the almonds are evenly golden all over.

4 Add to the salt mixture and toss together until the almonds are coated. Leave to cool, then store in a jar or airtight container for up to 1 week.

5 To serve the tapas, arrange in small, shallow serving dishes. Use fresh sprigs of tarragon to garnish the cheese and sprinkle the almonds with sea salt, if liked.

COOK'S TIP

If serving with pre-dinner drinks, provide cocktail sticks for spearing the olives and cheese.

DATES WITH CHORIZO

A delicious combination of fresh dates and spicy chorizo sausage is used for this tapas dish. Serve with a glass of good quality fino sherry.

INGREDIENTS

50g/2oz chorizo sausage
12 fresh dates, stoned
6 rashers streaky bacon
oil, for frying
plain flour, for dusting
1 egg, beaten
50g/2oz/1 cup fresh breadcrumbs

SERVES 4–6

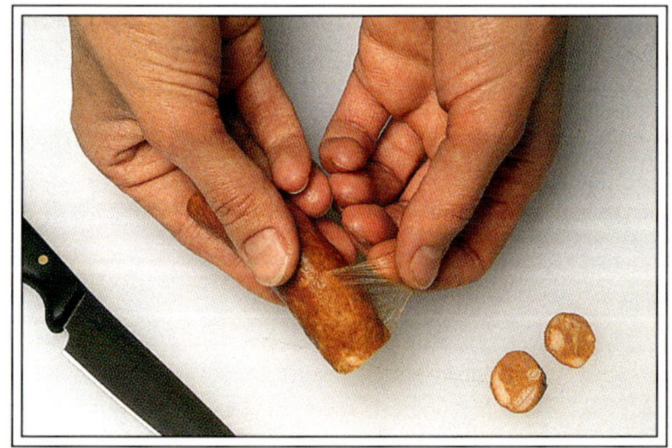

1 Trim the ends of the chorizo sausage, and peel away the skin. Cut into 2cm/¾in slices. Cut these in half lengthways, then in half again, giving 12 pieces.

2 Stuff each date with a piece of chorizo, closing the date around it. Stretch the bacon rashers, by running the back of a knife along the edge of the rasher, then cut each in half widthways. Wrap a piece of bacon around each date. Secure with a wooden cocktail stick.

3 Heat the oil in a deep pan; it should be at least 1cm/½in deep. Dust the dates with flour, then dip in the beaten egg, and finally coat in breadcrumbs. Fry in the hot oil, turning them, until golden. Remove with a slotted spoon and drain on kitchen paper. Serve immediately.

SPINACH EMPANADILLAS

These are little pastry turnovers, filled with ingredients that have a strong Moorish influence – pine nuts and raisins.

INGREDIENTS

25g/1oz/3 tbsp raisins
25ml/1½ tbsp olive oil
450g/1lb fresh spinach, washed and chopped
6 canned anchovies, drained and finely chopped
2 garlic cloves, finely chopped
25g/1oz/¼ cup pine nuts, chopped
350g/12oz ready-made puff pastry
1 egg, beaten
salt and ground black pepper

MAKES 20

1 To make the filling, soak the raisins in warm water for 10 minutes. Drain and roughly chop. Heat the oil in a large sauté pan or wok, add the spinach, stir, then cover and cook over a low heat for 2 minutes. Uncover, increase the heat and let any liquid evaporate. Add the seasoning, anchovies and garlic, and cook, stirring, for a further 1 minute. Remove from the heat, add the raisins and pine nuts, and leave to cool.

2 Preheat the oven to 180°C/350°F/Gas 4. Roll out the pastry on a floured surface to 3mm/⅛in thick. Using a 7.5cm/3in round pastry cutter, cut out 20 circles. Place 10ml/2 tsp filling in the middle of each circle, then brush the edges with water. Bring up the sides of the pastry and seal (*left*). Press the edges with a fork. Place on a greased baking sheet, brush with the egg and bake for about 15 minutes, until golden. Serve warm.

Spanish Omelette

Spanish omelette belongs in every cook's repertoire and can vary according to what you have in store. This version includes soft white beans and is finished with a layer of toasted sesame seeds.

Ingredients

30ml/2 tbsp olive oil
5ml/1 tsp sesame oil
1 Spanish onion, chopped
1 small red pepper, seeded and diced
2 celery sticks, chopped
400g/14oz can soft white beans, drained
8 eggs
45ml/3 tbsp sesame seeds
salt and ground black pepper
green salad, to serve

Serves 4

Variation

You can also use sliced cooked potatoes, any seasonal vegetables, baby artichoke hearts and chick-peas in a Spanish omelette.

1 Heat the olive oil and sesame oil in a 30cm/12in paella pan or frying pan. Add the onion, pepper and celery and cook until softened but not coloured.

2 Add the drained soft white beans to the pan, stir to combine, and cook gently over a low heat until the mixture is heated through.

3 In a large bowl, beat the eggs with a fork until well combined, season well with salt and ground black pepper and pour over the ingredients in the pan.

4 Stir in the egg mixture with a flat wooden spoon until it just begins to stiffen, then allow to firm over a low heat for about 6–8 minutes. Remove from the heat.

5 Preheat a moderate grill. Sprinkle the omelette with the sesame seeds and brown evenly under the grill. Watch to ensure that the seeds do not burn.

6 Cut the omelette into thick wedges and serve warm with a green salad. It is also delicious served cold.

GARLIC AND CHILLI PRAWNS

For this simple dish, you really need fresh raw prawns which absorb the flavours of the garlic and chilli as they fry. Have everything ready for last-minute cooking so you can take it to the table still sizzling.

INGREDIENTS

350–450g/12oz–1lb large raw prawns
2 red chillies
75ml/5 tbsp olive oil
3 garlic cloves, crushed
salt and ground black pepper

SERVES 4

1 Remove the heads and shells from the prawns, leaving the tails intact. Halve each chilli lengthways.

2 Heat the oil in a flameproof pan, suitable for serving. (Alternatively, use a frying pan and have a warmed serving dish ready in the oven.)

3 Add all the prawns, chilli and garlic to the pan and cook over a high heat for about 3 minutes, stirring, until the prawns turn pink. Season slightly and serve the prawns at once.

COOK'S TIP

The brief cooking time given is just sufficient for the chillies to flavour the juices produced by the prawns. Don't eat the chillies, though – they'll be really fiery hot!

Mediterranean Garlic Toasts

These garlic toasts are served as a starter in Spain. With a topping of plum tomatoes, mozzarella cheese and salami, they also make a filling snack.

Ingredients

150g/5oz mozzarella cheese, drained
2 plum tomatoes
½ French loaf
1 garlic clove, halved
30ml/2 tbsp olive oil, plus extra for brushing
12 small salami slices
15ml/1 tbsp fresh torn basil, or 5ml/1 tsp dried basil
salt and ground black pepper
fresh basil sprigs, to garnish

Serves 4

1 Preheat a moderate grill. Cut the mozzarella cheese into 12 slices and each tomato into six slices. Cut the French bread in half and slice each half horizontally.

2 Place the bread under the grill, cut-side up, and toast lightly. While the bread is still warm, rub the cut sides of the garlic on each cut side of the bread, then drizzle over about 7.5ml/½ tbsp of the olive oil.

3 Top each toast with three slices of salami, three slices of mozzarella and three slices of tomato. Brush the tops with a little more olive oil (*left*), season well and sprinkle over the fresh or dried basil.

4 Return to the grill and toast for about 3 minutes, until the cheese has melted. Remove and serve hot, garnished with sprigs of fresh basil.

Globe Artichokes with Beans and Alioli

As with the French *aïoli,* there are many recipes for the Spanish equivalent. The one used here is exceptionally garlicky, a perfect partner to freshly cooked vegetables.

Ingredients

For the Alioli

6 large garlic cloves, sliced
10ml/2 tsp white wine vinegar
250ml/8fl oz/1 cup olive oil
salt and ground black pepper

For the Salad

225g/8oz French beans
3 small globe artichokes
15ml/1 tbsp olive oil
pared rind of 1 lemon
coarse salt and ground black pepper, to sprinkle
lemon wedges, to garnish

Serves 4

Cook's Tip

To eat artichokes, the leaves should be pulled from the base and used to scoop a little sauce. It is the fleshy end of the leaf that is eaten. The base and heart of the artichoke can also be eaten.

1 To make the *alioli,* put the garlic and vinegar in a blender or mini food processor. With the machine running, gradually pour in the olive oil until the mixture is thickened and very smooth. (Alternatively, crush the garlic to a paste with the vinegar and gradually beat in the oil using a hand whisk.) Season to taste.

2 To make the salad, cook the beans in boiling water for 1–2 minutes until slightly softened. Drain.

3 Trim the artichoke stalks close to the base. Cook the artichokes in a large pan of boiling salted water for about 30 minutes or until you can easily pull away a leaf from the base. Drain well.

4 Halve the cooked artichokes lengthways with a sharp knife and carefully pull out the choke using a teaspoon.

5 Arrange the artichokes and beans on serving plates and drizzle with the oil. Scatter with the pared lemon rind and season with coarse salt and pepper. Spoon the *alioli* into the artichoke hearts and serve warm, garnished with lemon wedges.

Variation

Mediterranean baby artichokes are sometimes available and, unlike the larger ones, can be eaten whole. Cook until just tender, then simply cut in half to serve.

Canned artichoke hearts, thoroughly drained and sliced, may be substituted when fresh ones are not available.

PEPPER AND POTATO TORTILLA

This tortilla makes ideal picnic fare, as it is best eaten cold. Use a hard Spanish cheese, like Mahón, or a goat's cheese if you can, although mature Cheddar makes a good substitute.

INGREDIENTS

2 potatoes
1 green pepper
1 red pepper
45ml/3 tbsp olive oil
1 large onion, thinly sliced
2 garlic cloves, crushed
6 eggs, beaten
115g/4oz/1 cup grated mature cheese
salt and ground black pepper
15ml/1 tbsp chopped fresh parsley, to garnish

SERVES 4

VARIATION

You can add any sliced and lightly cooked vegetable, such as mushrooms, courgettes or broccoli, to this tortilla dish instead of peppers. Cooked pasta or brown rice are both excellent alternatives too.

1 Do not peel the potatoes, but wash them thoroughly, then par-boil them for about 10 minutes. Drain and slice thickly. Preheat a hot grill.

2 Remove the stalks from the green and red peppers, seed them and cut into thin slices. In a large non-stick frying pan, heat the oil and fry the onion, garlic and peppers over a moderate heat for 5 minutes until softened.

3 Add the potatoes and continue frying, stirring occasionally, until the potatoes are completely cooked and the vegetables are soft. Add a little extra oil if the pan seems too dry.

4 Pour in half the eggs and sprinkle over half the grated cheese, then add the rest of the egg, seasoning as you go. Finish with a layer of cheese.

5 Continue to cook over a low heat, without stirring, half covering the pan with a lid to help set the eggs.

6 When the mixture is firm, place the pan under the hot grill to lightly seal the top. Leave the tortilla in the pan to cool. This helps it firm up further and makes it easier to turn out. Garnish with parsley.

Spanish Chilli Potatoes

The Spanish name for this dish, *Patatas Bravas*, means "fierce, hot potatoes". You can always reduce the amount of chilli to suit your taste.

Ingredients

1kg/2¼lb new or salad potatoes
60ml/4 tbsp olive oil
1 onion, finely chopped
2 garlic cloves, crushed
15ml/1 tbsp tomato purée
200g/7oz can chopped tomatoes
15ml/1 tbsp red wine vinegar
2–3 small dried red chillies, seeded and chopped finely, or 5–10ml/1–2 tsp hot chilli powder
5ml/1 tsp paprika
salt and ground black pepper
flat leaf parsley sprig, to garnish

Serves 4

1 Boil the potatoes in their skins for about 10–12 minutes or until they are just tender. Drain well through a colander and leave to cool, then cut in half and reserve until needed.

2 Heat the oil in a large pan and add the onion and garlic. Fry gently for about 5–6 minutes. Stir in the tomato purée, tomatoes, vinegar, chillies or chilli powder and paprika; simmer for about 5 minutes.

3 Add the potatoes and mix to coat well. Cover and simmer for 8–10 minutes, or until the potatoes are tender. Season and transfer to a warmed serving dish. Serve garnished with a sprig of flat leaf parsley.

Mediterranean Mixed Pepper Salad

This cheerful and tasty dish could be brightened up further by using orange and green peppers too, although green peppers do not have such a sweet flavour.

Ingredients

2 red peppers, halved and seeded
2 yellow peppers, halved and seeded
150ml/¼ pint/⅔ cup olive oil
1 onion, thinly sliced
2 garlic cloves, crushed
squeeze of lemon juice
salt and ground black pepper
chopped fresh parsley, to garnish

Serves 4

1 Grill the red and yellow pepper halves for 5 minutes, until the skins have blistered and blackened. Put them into a plastic bag, seal and leave for 5 minutes.

2 Meanwhile, heat 30ml/2 tbsp of the olive oil in a frying pan and add the onion. Fry for 5–6 minutes, until the onion is softened and translucent. Remove from the heat and reserve until needed.

3 Take the peppers out of the bag and peel off the skins. Discard the pepper skins and slice the peppers into fairly thin strips.

4 Place the peppers, cooked onions and any oil from the pan into a bowl. Add the crushed garlic and pour on the remaining olive oil, add a good squeeze of lemon juice and season. Mix well, cover and marinate for 2–3 hours, stirring the mixture once or twice.

5 Garnish the mixed pepper salad with chopped fresh parsley and serve as an accompaniment to cold meats.

Cook's Tip

This salad also makes a delicious starter, served with crusty bread.

Spanish Beans with Ham

The Spanish name for this dish is *Judias verdes con jamón*. French beans are cooked with Spanish raw-cured dried Serrano ham. Garlic and onion provide extra flavour.

Ingredients

450g/1lb French beans
45ml/3 tbsp olive oil
1 onion, thinly sliced
2 garlic cloves, finely chopped
75g/3oz Serrano ham, chopped
salt and ground black pepper

Serves 4

1 Cook the French beans in a large saucepan of boiling salted water for about 5–6 minutes, until *al dente*.

2 Meanwhile, heat the oil in a pan, add the onion and fry for 5 minutes, until softened and translucent. Add the garlic and ham and cook for a further 1–2 minutes.

3 Drain the beans, add to the pan and cook, stirring occasionally, for about 2–3 minutes. Season well with salt and ground black pepper and serve hot.

Cook's Tip

If you cannot find Serrano ham, substitute Parma ham or even unsmoked bacon in this simple dish.

AVOCADO, ORANGE AND ALMOND SALAD

The flavours and textures in this colourful and refreshing salad mix to make a well-balanced dish.

INGREDIENTS

2 oranges
2 well-flavoured tomatoes
2 small avocados
60ml/4 tbsp extra virgin olive oil
30ml/2 tbsp lemon juice
15ml/1 tbsp chopped fresh parsley
1 small onion, sliced into rings
salt and ground black pepper
25g/1oz/¼ cup flaked almonds and
12 black olives, to garnish

SERVES 4

OPPOSITE TOP: *Fresh broad bean salad*
OPPOSITE BELOW: *Avocado, orange and almond salad*

1 Peel the oranges, and slice into thick rounds. Plunge the tomatoes into boiling water for 30 seconds, then refresh in cold water. Peel away the skins, cut into quarters, remove the seeds, and cut the flesh into chunks.

2 Cut the avocados in half, remove the stones, and carefully peel away the skin. Cut into chunks.

3 Mix together the olive oil, lemon juice and chopped fresh parsley. Season with salt and black pepper. Toss the avocado and tomato in half of the dressing.

4 Arrange the sliced oranges on a serving plate and scatter the onion rings on top. Drizzle with the remaining dressing. Pile the avocado and tomato mixture in the middle of the plate. Garnish with the flaked almonds and black olives.

FRESH BROAD BEAN SALAD

Broad beans are used in fresh and dried form in Spain. This salad could be served either as a starter or as a lunch dish.

INGREDIENTS

225g/8oz shelled broad beans
175g/6oz chorizo sausage
60ml/4 tbsp extra virgin olive oil
225g/8oz brown cap mushrooms, sliced
15ml/1 tbsp snipped fresh chives
salt and ground black pepper

SERVES 4

1 Cook the broad beans in boiling salted water for 7–8 minutes. Drain and refresh under cold water. If the beans are large, peel away the tough outer skins.

2 Remove the skin from the chorizo sausage, and cut it into small chunks. Heat the oil in a frying pan. Add the chorizo, and cook for 2–3 minutes. Add the warm chorizo to the mushrooms, with any extra oil in the pan, and mix well. Leave to cool.

3 Stir the broad beans and chives into the mushroom and sausage mixture, and season with salt and ground black pepper. Serve at room temperature.

HAKE WITH MUSSELS

Cod and haddock cutlets will work just as well as hake in this tasty fish dish, with its delicious sauce containing both wine and sherry.

INGREDIENTS

30ml/2 tbsp olive oil
25g/1oz/2 tbsp butter
1 onion, chopped
3 garlic cloves, crushed
15ml/1 tbsp plain flour
2.5ml/½ tsp paprika
4 hake cutlets, about 175g/6oz each
225g/8oz French beans, cut into 2.5cm/1in lengths
350ml/12fl oz/1½ cups fish stock
150ml/¼ pint/⅔ cup dry white wine
30ml/2 tbsp dry sherry
16–20 live mussels, cleaned
45ml/3 tbsp chopped fresh parsley
salt and ground black pepper
crusty bread, to serve

SERVES 4

1 Heat the oil and butter in a frying pan, add the onion and cook for 5 minutes, until softened. Add the crushed garlic and cook for a further 1 minute.

2 Mix together the plain flour and paprika, then lightly dust over the hake cutlets. Push the onion and garlic mixture to one side of the frying pan, then add the hake cutlets to the pan and fry until golden on both sides.

3 Stir in the beans, fish stock, white wine and sherry, and season to taste. Bring to the boil and cook the fish over a low heat for about 2 minutes.

4 Discard any mussels that remain open when tapped. Add the mussels and parsley, cover and cook for 8 minutes. (Discard any mussels that do not open.)

5 Serve the hake in warmed, shallow soup plates with plenty of crusty bread to mop up the juices.

CHUNKY SEAFOOD STEW

This is a versatile stew in which many different combinations of fish and shellfish may be used. Only ever buy absolutely fresh fish.

INGREDIENTS

45ml/3 tbsp olive oil
2 large onions, chopped
1 small green pepper, seeded and sliced
3 carrots, chopped
3 garlic cloves, crushed
30ml/2 tbsp tomato purée
2 x 400g/14oz cans chopped tomatoes
45ml/3 tbsp chopped fresh parsley
5ml/1 tsp fresh thyme, or 1.5ml/¼ tsp dried thyme
15ml/1 tbsp chopped fresh basil, or 5ml/1 tsp dried basil
120ml/4fl oz/½ cup dry white wine
450g/1lb raw prawns, peeled and deveined, or cooked peeled prawns
1.5kg/3–3½lb live mussels or clams, or a mixture of both, thoroughly cleaned
900g/2lb halibut or other firm, white fish fillets, cut into 5–7.5cm/2–3in pieces
350ml/12fl oz/1½ cups fish stock or water
salt and ground black pepper
chopped fresh herbs, to garnish

SERVES 6

1 Heat the oil in a flameproof casserole. Add the onions, green pepper, carrots and garlic and cook until the vegetables are tender, about 5 minutes.

2 Add the tomato purée, canned tomatoes, herbs and wine and stir well to combine. Bring to the boil and simmer for 20 minutes.

3 Add the raw prawns, if using, mussels or clams, fish pieces and stock or water. Season with salt and pepper.

4 Bring back to the boil, then simmer for about 5–6 minutes, until the prawns turn pink, the fish flakes easily and the mussels and clams open. If using cooked prawns, add these for the last 2 minutes.

5 Ladle into large, warmed soup plates and serve garnished with a sprinkling of chopped fresh herbs.

COOK'S TIP

Before cooking, discard any shellfish that remain open when tapped. After cooking, discard any that remain closed.

ZARZUELA

Zarzuela means "light opera" or "musical comedy" and the classic fish stew of the same name should be as lively and colourful as the *Zarzuela* itself. This feast of fish includes lobster and other shellfish, but you can always vary the ingredients if you wish.

INGREDIENTS

1 cooked lobster
24 live mussels or clams
1 large monkfish tail, skinned
225g/8oz squid rings
15ml/1 tbsp plain flour
90ml/6 tbsp olive oil
12 large raw prawns
2 large mild onions, chopped
4 garlic cloves, crushed
30ml/2 tbsp brandy
450g/1lb ripe tomatoes, peeled and roughly chopped
2 bay leaves
5ml/1 tsp paprika
1 red chilli, seeded and chopped
300ml/½ pint/1¼ cups fish stock
15g/½oz/2 tbsp ground almonds
30ml/2 tbsp chopped fresh parsley
salt and ground black pepper
green salad and warm bread, to serve

SERVES 6

1 Using a large knife, cut the lobster in half lengthways. Remove the dark intestine. Crack the claws using a hammer.

2 Scrub the mussels or clams; discard any that are damaged or remain open when tapped. Cut the monkfish fillets from the central cartilage and cut each fillet into

3 Toss the monkfish and squid rings in seasoned flour. Fry quickly in the oil on all sides. Drain and fry the raw prawns on both sides, then drain.

4 Fry the onions and two-thirds of the garlic for 3 minutes. Add the brandy and ignite with a taper. When the flames die down add the tomatoes, bay leaves, paprika, chilli and stock.

5 Bring to the boil, reduce the heat and simmer gently for 5 minutes. Add the mussels or clams, cover and cook for 3–4 minutes until the shells open.

6 Remove the mussels or clams from the sauce and discard any shells which remain closed.

7 Arrange all the fish and lobster in a large flameproof serving dish. Blend the almonds to a paste with the remaining garlic and parsley and stir into the sauce.

8 Pour the sauce over the fish and cook gently for 5 minutes until hot. Add the cooked prawns and heat through. Serve with a green salad and lots of warm bread.

COOK'S TIP

Take the serving dish to the table and ladle out the portions, making sure everyone gets a taste of all the different types of seafood.

FISH FILLETS WITH ORANGE AND TOMATO SAUCE

A slightly spicy and colourful sauce complements tender white fish fillets in this flavoursome dish.

INGREDIENTS

20g/¾oz/3 tbsp plain flour
4 fillets firm white fish such as cod, sea bass or sole, about 175g/6oz each
15g/½oz/1 tbsp butter or margarine
30ml/2 tbsp olive oil
1 onion, sliced
2 garlic cloves, chopped
1.5ml/¼ tsp ground cumin
500g/1¼lb tomatoes, peeled, seeded and chopped, or 400g/14oz can chopped tomatoes
120ml/4fl oz/½ cup fresh orange juice
salt and ground black pepper
orange wedges, to garnish
mange-touts, to serve

SERVES 4

1 Put the flour on a plate and season with salt and pepper. Coat the fish fillets with the flour, shaking off any excess.

2 Heat the butter or margarine and half of the oil in a large frying pan. Add the fish fillets to the pan and cook for about 3 minutes on each side until the fish is golden and the flesh flakes easily when tested.

3 When the fish is cooked, transfer to a warmed serving plate. Cover with foil and keep warm while making the sauce.

4 Heat the remaining oil in the pan. Add the onion and garlic and cook until softened, about 5 minutes.

5 Stir in the cumin, tomatoes and orange juice. Bring to the boil and cook for about 10 minutes, stirring, until thickened.

6 Garnish the fish with orange wedges and serve with mange-touts. Hand the sauce round separately.

Grilled King Prawns

Romesco sauce, from the Catalan region of Spain, is served with these prawns. It can also be used to accompany other fish and seafood.

INGREDIENTS

24 raw king prawns in the shell
30–45ml/2–3 tbsp olive oil

FOR THE *ROMESCO* SAUCE

2 well-flavoured tomatoes
60ml/4 tbsp olive oil
1 onion, chopped
4 garlic cloves, chopped
1 canned pimiento, drained and chopped
2.5ml/½ tsp dried chilli flakes
75ml/5 tbsp fish stock
30ml/2 tbsp dry white wine
10 blanched almonds, toasted
15ml/1 tbsp red wine vinegar
salt, to taste
lemon wedges and flat leaf parsley, to garnish

SERVES 4

1 Slash the bottoms of the tomatoes with a sharp knife. Immerse them in boiling water for 30 seconds, then refresh under cold water. Peel off the skins and roughly chop the flesh.

2 Heat 30ml/2 tbsp of the oil in a pan, add the onion and three cloves of garlic, and cook until soft. Add the chopped pimiento and tomato, with the chilli flakes, stock and wine. Cover and simmer for 30 minutes.

3 Put the almonds in a blender or food processor and grind coarsely. Add the remaining oil and garlic, and the vinegar. Process until combined. Add the tomato sauce and process until smooth.

4 Remove the heads from the prawns and, with a sharp knife, slit each one down the back and remove the black vein. Rinse under cold running water and pat dry on kitchen paper.

5 Preheat the grill. Toss the prawns in olive oil, then grill for about 2–3 minutes on each side, until pink. Arrange on a plate, garnish with lemon wedges and parsley and serve the sauce in a small bowl.

SEAFOOD PAELLA

Bring the paella pan to the table and let everyone help themselves – for informal entertaining at its easiest and most relaxed.

INGREDIENTS

60ml/4 tbsp olive oil
225g/8oz monkfish or cod, skinned and cut into chunks
3 prepared baby squid, body cut into rings and tentacles chopped
1 red mullet, filleted, skinned and cut into chunks (optional)
1 onion, chopped
3 garlic cloves, finely chopped
1 red pepper, seeded and sliced
4 tomatoes, skinned and chopped
225g/8oz/generous 1 cup arborio rice
450ml/¾ pint/1⅞ cups fish stock
150ml/¼ pint/⅔ cup white wine
75g/3oz/¾ cup frozen peas
4–5 saffron strands soaked in 30ml/2 tbsp hot water
115g/4oz/1 cup cooked peeled prawns
8 live mussels, cleaned
salt and ground black pepper
15ml/1 tbsp chopped fresh parsley, to garnish
lemon slices, to serve

SERVES 4

1 Heat 30ml/2 tbsp of the oil in a paella pan or large frying pan and add the monkfish or cod, the squid and the red mullet, if using, to the pan. Stir-fry for 2 minutes, then transfer the fish to a bowl with all the juices and reserve.

2 Heat the remaining 30ml/2 tbsp of oil in the pan and add the onion, garlic and pepper. Fry for 6–7 minutes, stirring frequently, until the onions and peppers have softened.

3 Stir in the tomatoes and fry for about 2 minutes, then add the rice, stirring to coat the grains with oil, and cook for 2–3 minutes. Pour on the fish stock and wine and add the peas, saffron and the soaking water. Season well and mix.

4 Gently stir in the reserved cooked fish and squid with all the juices, followed by the prawns, then push the mussels into the rice. Cover and cook over a gentle heat for about 30 minutes, or until the stock has been absorbed by the rice but the mixture is still moist. Discard any unopened mussels.

5 Remove from the heat, keep covered and leave to stand for 5 minutes. Sprinkle with chopped fresh parsley and serve with lemon slices for squeezing over.

BLACK BEAN STEW

This simple stew uses a few robust ingredients to create a deliciously intense flavour – the Spanish equivalent of a French cassoulet.

INGREDIENTS

275g/10oz/generous 1½ cups dried black beans
675g/1½lb boneless belly pork rashers
60ml/4 tbsp olive oil
350g/12oz baby onions
2 celery sticks, thinly sliced
10ml/2 tsp paprika
150g/5oz chorizo sausage, cut into chunks
600ml/1 pint/2½ cups light chicken or vegetable stock
2 green peppers, seeded and cut into large pieces
salt and ground black pepper

SERVES 5–6

COOK'S TIP

This is the sort of stew to which you can add a variety of winter vegetables such as chunks of leek, turnip, celeriac and even little potatoes.

1 Put the beans in a bowl and cover with plenty of cold water. Leave to soak overnight. Drain the beans, place in a saucepan and cover with fresh water. Bring to the boil and boil rapidly for 10 minutes. Drain through a colander.

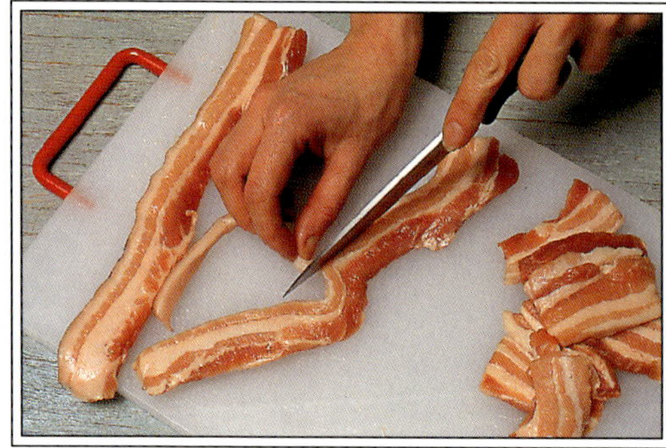

2 Preheat the oven to 160°C/325°F/Gas 3. Cut away any rind from the pork and cut the meat into large chunks.

3 Heat the oil in a large frying pan and fry the onions and celery for 3 minutes. Add the pork and fry for 5–10 minutes until the pork is browned all over.

4 Add the paprika and chorizo and fry for a further 2 minutes. Transfer to an ovenproof dish with the black beans and mix together well.

5 Add the stock to the pan and bring to the boil. Season lightly then pour over the meat and beans. Cover and bake in the oven for 1 hour.

6 Stir the green peppers into the stew, then cover and return to the oven for a further 15 minutes. Serve hot.

Chicken Paella

There are many variations of this basic recipe. Any seasonal vegetables can be added, as can mussels and other shellfish. Serve straight from the pan.

Ingredients

4 chicken legs (thighs and drumsticks)
60ml/4 tbsp olive oil
1 large onion, finely chopped
1 garlic clove, crushed
5ml/1 tsp ground turmeric
115g/4oz chorizo sausage or smoked ham
225g/8oz/generous 1 cup long grain rice
600ml/1 pint/2½ cups chicken stock
4 tomatoes, skinned, seeded and chopped
1 red pepper, seeded and sliced
115g/4oz/1 cup frozen peas
salt and ground black pepper

Serves 4

1 Preheat the oven to 180°C/350°F/Gas 4. Cut the chicken legs in half through the joints to give eight pieces.

2 Heat the oil in a 30cm/12in paella pan or large flameproof casserole and brown the chicken pieces on both sides. Add the onion and garlic and stir in the turmeric. Cook for 2 minutes.

3 Slice the chorizo sausage or dice the smoked ham and add to the pan with the rice and chicken stock. Bring to the boil and season to taste with salt and pepper, cover and bake for 15 minutes.

4 Remove from the oven and add the chopped tomatoes, sliced red pepper and frozen peas. Return to the oven and cook for a further 10–15 minutes or until the chicken is tender and the stock absorbed.

CHICKEN WITH CHORIZO

The addition of chorizo sausage and Spanish sherry gives a warm and interesting flavour to this dish.

INGREDIENTS

1.5kg/3–3½lb chicken, jointed, or
4 chicken legs, halved and skinned
10ml/2 tsp paprika
60ml/4 tbsp olive oil
2 small onions, sliced
6 garlic cloves, thinly sliced
150g/5oz chorizo sausage, thickly sliced
400g/14oz can chopped tomatoes
2 bay leaves
75ml/3fl oz/⅓ cup medium sherry
salt and ground black pepper
boiled potatoes, to serve

SERVES 4

1 Preheat the oven to 190°C/375°F/Gas 5. Coat the chicken pieces in the paprika and season lightly with salt.

2 Heat the olive oil in a frying pan and fry the chicken on all sides to brown. With a slotted spoon, transfer the chicken pieces to an ovenproof dish.

3 Add the onions to the pan and fry quickly until golden. Add the garlic and chorizo and fry for 2 minutes. (Don't burn the garlic, or it will taste bitter.)

VARIATION

Use pork chump chops or leg steaks instead of the chicken and reduce the cooking time slightly.

4 Add the tomatoes, bay leaves and sherry and bring to the boil. Pour over the chicken and cover with a lid. Bake in the oven for 45 minutes. Remove the lid and season to taste with salt and pepper. Cook for a further 20 minutes until the chicken is tender and golden. Serve with potatoes.

CHICKEN WITH HAM AND RICE

This colourful one-pan dish is ideal for entertaining as it needs no last-minute preparation. Serve with a crisp mixed green salad.

INGREDIENTS

15g/½oz/2 tbsp plain flour
10ml/2 tsp paprika
2.5ml/½ tsp salt
16 chicken drumsticks
60ml/4 tbsp olive oil
1.2 litres/2 pints/5 cups chicken stock
1 onion, finely chopped
2 garlic cloves, crushed
450g/1lb/generous 2¼ cups long grain rice
2 bay leaves
225g/8oz/2 cups diced cooked ham
115g/4oz/1 cup pimiento-stuffed green olives
1 green pepper, seeded and diced
2 x 400g/14oz cans chopped tomatoes, with their juice
parsley sprigs, to garnish

SERVES 8

1 Preheat the oven to 180°C/350°F/Gas 4. Shake together the flour, paprika and salt in a plastic bag, add the drumsticks and toss to coat all over.

2 Heat the oil in a large flameproof casserole and, working in batches, brown the chicken slowly on all sides. Remove and keep warm.

3 Meanwhile, bring the stock to the boil and add the onion, crushed garlic, rice and bay leaves. Cook for 10 minutes. Draw aside and add the ham, olives, pepper and canned tomatoes with their juice. Transfer to a shallow ovenproof dish.

4 Arrange the chicken on top, cover and bake for 30–40 minutes or until tender. Add a little more stock if necessary to prevent drying out. Remove the bay leaves and serve garnished with parsley.

Rabbit Salmorejo

Small pieces of jointed rabbit, conveniently sold in packs from the supermarket, make an interesting alternative to chicken in this light, spicy sauté. Serve with a simply dressed salad.

Ingredients

675g/1½lb rabbit portions
300ml/½ pint/1¼ cups dry white wine
15ml/1 tbsp sherry vinegar
several sprigs of fresh oregano
2 bay leaves
90ml/6 tbsp olive oil
175g/6oz baby onions, peeled and left whole
1 red chilli, seeded and finely chopped
4 garlic cloves, sliced
10ml/2 tsp paprika
150ml/¼ pint/⅔ cup chicken stock
salt and ground black pepper
flat leaf parsley sprigs, to garnish (optional)

Serves 4

Cook's Tip

If more convenient, transfer the stew to an ovenproof dish and bake at 180°C/350°F/Gas 4 for 50 minutes, or until the meat is tender.

1 Put the rabbit in a bowl. Add the wine, vinegar and herbs and toss together lightly. Cover and leave to marinate for several hours or overnight.

2 Drain the rabbit, reserving the marinade, and pat dry on kitchen paper. Heat the oil in a large sauté or frying pan. Add the rabbit and fry on all sides until golden. Drain well. Then fry the onions until just beginning to colour.

3 Remove the onions from the pan and add the chilli, garlic and paprika. Cook, stirring, for 1 minute. Add the reserved marinade, stock and a little seasoning.

4 Return the rabbit to the pan with the onions. Bring to the boil, reduce the heat and cover with a lid. Simmer very gently for about 45 minutes until the rabbit is tender. Serve the *salmorejo* garnished with sprigs of fresh parsley, if using.

CHICKEN CASSEROLE WITH SPICED FIGS

The Catalans have various recipes for fruit with meat, and this is an unusual dish which uses fresh figs.

INGREDIENTS

FOR THE FIGS

150g/5oz/¾ cup granulated sugar
120ml/4fl oz/½ cup white wine vinegar
1 slice lemon
1 cinnamon stick
450g/1lb fresh figs

FOR THE CHICKEN

120ml/4fl oz/½ cup medium sweet white wine
rind of ½ lemon
1.5kg/3–3½lb chicken, jointed into eight pieces
50g/2oz lardons or thick streaky bacon, cut into strips
15ml/1 tbsp olive oil
50ml/2fl oz/¼ cup chicken stock
salt and ground black pepper
green salad, to serve (optional)

SERVES 4

1 Bring 120ml/4fl oz/½ cup water to the boil with the sugar, vinegar, lemon and cinnamon. Simmer for 5 minutes. Add the figs; simmer for 10 minutes. Remove from the heat, cover, and set aside overnight.

2 Preheat the oven to 180°C/350°F/Gas 4. Drain the figs and place in a bowl. Add the wine and lemon rind. Season the chicken. In a large, shallow ovenproof dish, cook the lardons or bacon until the fat runs, and they turn golden. Remove, leaving the oil in the pan. Add the olive oil and brown the chicken pieces all over.

3 Strain the figs and add the wine to the chicken. Boil until reduced and syrupy. Transfer the dish to the oven and cook, uncovered, for 20 minutes. Add the figs and chicken stock, cover the dish, and return to the oven for about a further 10 minutes. Serve the chicken and figs with a green salad, if liked.

Pork and Sausage Casserole

Another pork dish from Catalonia, that uses the spicy *butifarra* sausage. This can be found in some Spanish delicatessens but, if not, sweet Italian sausage will do.

Ingredients

30ml/2 tbsp olive oil
4 boneless pork chops, about 175g/6oz each
4 butifarra *or sweet Italian sausages*
1 onion, chopped
2 cloves garlic, chopped
120ml/4fl oz/½ cup dry white wine
4 plum tomatoes, chopped
1 bay leaf
15ml/1 tbsp chopped fresh parsley
salt and ground black pepper

Serves 4

1 Preheat the oven to 180°C/350°F/Gas 4. Heat the oil in a frying pan. Brown the pork chops on both sides (*left*), transfer to a plate and keep warm. Add the sausages, onion and garlic to the pan, cook until the sausages are browned and the onion is soft.

2 Stir in the wine, tomatoes and bay leaf, and season with salt and pepper. Add the parsley. Transfer to an ovenproof dish, cover, and bake for about 30 minutes. Slice the sausages, and serve immediately with the chops.

SPICED DUCK WITH PEARS

This delicious casserole is based on a Catalan dish that uses goose or duck. The sautéed pears are added towards the end of cooking along with *picarda* sauce, a pounded pine nut and garlic paste which both flavours and thickens the dish.

INGREDIENTS

6 duck portions, either breast or leg
15ml/1 tbsp olive oil
1 large onion, thinly sliced
1 cinnamon stick, halved
2 thyme sprigs
450ml/¾ pint/1⅞ cups chicken stock

TO FINISH

3 firm, ripe pears
30ml/2 tbsp olive oil
2 garlic cloves, sliced
25g/1oz/¼ cup pine nuts
2.5ml/½ tsp saffron strands
25g/1oz/3 tbsp raisins
salt and ground black pepper
parsley or thyme sprigs, to garnish
mashed potatoes, to serve

SERVES 6

1 Preheat the oven to 180°C/350°F/Gas 4. Fry the duck portions in the oil for about 5 minutes until the skin is golden. Transfer the duck to an ovenproof dish and drain off all but 15ml/1 tbsp of the fat left in the pan.

2 Add the sliced onion to the pan and fry for 5 minutes. Add the cinnamon stick, thyme and stock and bring to the boil. Pour over the duck portions and bake in the oven for 1¼ hours.

COOK'S TIP

A good stock is essential for this dish. Buy a large duck (plus two extra duck breasts if you want generous portions) and joint it yourself, using the giblets and carcass to make stock. Alternatively, buy duck portions and a carton of fresh chicken stock.

3 Meanwhile, halve the pears and fry quickly in the oil until they begin to turn golden on the cut sides. Using a pestle and mortar, pound the garlic, pine nuts and saffron to make a thick, smooth paste.

4 Add the paste to the casserole along with the raisins and pears. Bake in the oven for a further 15 minutes until the pear halves are tender.

5 Season to taste and garnish with parsley or thyme. Serve the duck hot, with mashed potatoes.

CHOCOLATE AND ORANGE CAKE

This light-as-air sponge, with its fluffy icing, tastes absolutely heavenly and will round off an elegant dinner perfectly.

INGREDIENTS

25g/1oz/¼ cup plain flour
15g/½oz/2 tbsp cocoa powder
15g/½oz/2 tbsp cornflour
pinch of salt
5 egg whites
2.5ml/½ tsp cream of tartar
115g/4oz/generous ½ cup caster sugar
blanched and shredded rind of 1 orange, to decorate

FOR THE ICING

200g/7oz/1 cup caster sugar
1 egg white

SERVES 10

1 Preheat the oven to 180°C/350°F/Gas 4. Sift the flour, cocoa powder, cornflour and salt together three times into a bowl. Beat the egg whites in a large bowl until foamy. Add the cream of tartar, then whisk until soft peaks form.

2 Add the caster sugar to the egg whites a spoonful at a time, whisking after each addition. Sift a third of the flour and cocoa mixture over the meringue and gently fold in. Repeat, sifting and folding in the flour and cocoa mixture two more times.

3 Spoon the mixture into a non-stick 20cm/8in ring mould and level the top. Bake in the oven for 35 minutes or until springy when pressed lightly. Turn upside-down on to a wire rack and leave to cool in the tin. Carefully ease out of the tin.

4 For the icing, put the sugar in a pan with 75ml/5 tbsp water. Stir over a low heat to dissolve. Boil until the syrup reaches 120°C/250°F on a sugar thermometer, or when a drop of syrup makes a soft ball when dropped into cold water. Take off the heat.

5 Whisk the egg white until stiff. Add the syrup in a thin stream, whisking all the time. Continue to whisk until the mixture is very thick and fluffy. Spread the icing over the top and sides of the cake. Sprinkle with the orange rind and serve.

CHURROS

These doughnuts are commercially deep fried in huge coils and broken off into smaller lengths for selling. Serve this home-made version freshly cooked with hot chocolate or strong coffee.

INGREDIENTS

200g/7oz/1¾ cups plain flour
1.5ml/¼ tsp salt
30ml/2 tbsp caster sugar
60ml/4 tbsp olive or sunflower oil
1 egg, beaten
caster sugar and ground cinnamon, for dusting
oil, for deep frying

MAKES 12–15

1 Sift the flour, salt and sugar on to a plate or piece of paper. Heat 250ml/8fl oz/1 cup water in a saucepan with the oil until just boiling.

2 Tip in the flour and beat with a wooden spoon until the mixture forms a stiff paste. Leave to cool for 2 minutes.

3 Gradually beat in the egg until smooth. Oil a large baking sheet. Sprinkle plenty of sugar on to a plate and stir in a little ground cinnamon.

4 Put the dough in a large piping bag fitted with a 1cm/½in plain piping nozzle. Pipe little coils or S-shapes on to the prepared baking sheet.

5 Heat a 5cm/2in depth of oil in a large, deep-sided saucepan to 168°C/336°F, or until a little spare dough dropped in sizzles on the surface.

6 Using an oiled fish slice, lower several of the piped shapes into the oil and cook for about 2 minutes until light golden.

7 Drain on kitchen paper then coat with the sugar and cinnamon mixture. Keep warm. Cook the remainder in the same way and serve the *churros* immediately.

Crema Catalana

This delicious pudding is a cross between a *crème caramel* and a *crème brûlée*. It is not as rich as a *crème brûlée* but has a similar caramelized sugar topping.

Ingredients

475ml/16fl oz/2 cups milk
rind of ½ lemon
1 cinnamon stick
4 egg yolks
105ml/7 tbsp caster sugar
25ml/1½ tbsp cornflour
grated nutmeg, for sprinkling

Serves 4

1 Put the milk in a pan with the lemon rind and cinnamon stick. Bring to the boil and simmer for 10 minutes then remove the rind and cinnamon. Whisk the egg yolks and 45ml/3 tbsp of the sugar until pale yellow. Add the cornflour and mix well.

2 Stir in a few tablespoons of the hot milk, then add this mixture to the remaining milk. Return to the heat and cook gently, stirring, for about 5 minutes, until thickened and smooth. Do not let it boil. There should be no cornflour taste.

3 Pour the custard mixture into four shallow ovenproof dishes, about 13cm/5in in diameter. Leave to cool completely, then chill in the fridge, overnight if possible, until firm.

4 Before serving, preheat a grill. Sprinkle each dish with 15ml/1 tbsp sugar and a little grated nutmeg. Place the puddings under the grill, on the highest shelf, and grill until the sugar caramelizes. This will only take a few seconds. Leave the puddings to cool for a few minutes before serving. (The caramelized topping will only stay hard for about 30 minutes.)

ORANGE SORBET

These little orange sorbets look very pretty served in the fruit shells. They are easy to make – and even easier to eat.

INGREDIENTS

150g/5oz/¾ cup granulated sugar
juice of 1 lemon
14 oranges
8 fresh bay leaves, to decorate

SERVES 8

1 Put the sugar in a heavy-based pan. Add half the lemon juice and 120ml/4fl oz/ ½ cup water. Cook over a low heat until the sugar has dissolved. Bring to the boil and boil for 2–3 minutes, until the syrup is clear. Leave to cool.

2 With a sharp knife, slice the tops off eight of the oranges, to make "hats" for the sorbets. Scoop out the flesh of the oranges into a bowl and reserve. Put the orange shells and "hats" on a tray and place in the freezer until needed.

3 Grate the rind of the remaining oranges and add to the syrup. Squeeze the juice from the oranges and the reserved flesh. There should be 750ml/1¼ pints/3 cups. (If necessary, make up with bought fresh orange juice, or squeeze another orange.)

4 Stir all the freshly squeezed orange juice and the rest of the lemon juice, plus 90ml/6 tbsp cold water, into the sugar syrup. Taste, and add more lemon juice or granulated sugar if you need to. Pour the mixture into a shallow, freezer-proof container and place in the freezer for 3 hours.

5 Turn the mixture into a bowl and beat with a whisk to break down the ice crystals. Return to the container and freeze for 4 hours, until firm but not solid. Pack the mixture into the orange shells, mounding it up, and set the "hats" on top.

6 Store the oranges in the freezer until ready to serve. Just before serving, push a skewer into the tops of the "hats" and insert a bay leaf into each one.

INDEX